BELTER/MEZZO-SOPRANO

BERNSTEIN FOR SINGERS

10 SONGS

T0101667

To access companion recorded accompaniments online, visit:
www.halleonard.com/mylibrary

Enter Code
4669-0714-0939-0947

ISBN 978-1-4803-6447-9

The Name and Likeness of "Leonard Bernstein" is a registered trademark of Amberson Holdings LLC.
Used by Permission

LEONARD
BERNSTEIN
Music Publishing
Company LLC

BOOSEY&HAWKES

AN IMAGEM COMPANY

DISTRIBUTED BY

HAL•LEONARD®
CORPORATION
7777 W. BLUEMOUND RD. P.O. BOX 13819 MILWAUKEE, WI 53213

Copyright © 2015 by Boosey & Hawkes, Inc.
All Rights Reserved

For all works contained herein:
Unauthorized copying, arranging, adapting, recording, Internet posting, public performance,
or other distribution of the printed music in this publication is an infringement of copyright.
Infringers are liable under the law.

www.leonardbernstein.com
www.boosey.com
www.halleonard.com

LEONARD BERNSTEIN
August 25, 1918 - October 14, 1990

Leonard Bernstein was born in Lawrence, Massachusetts. He took piano lessons as a boy and attended the Garrison and Boston Latin Schools. At Harvard University he studied with Walter Piston, Edward Burlingame-Hill, and A. Tillman Merritt, among others. Before graduating in 1939 he made an unofficial conducting debut with his own incidental music to the Aristophanes play *The Birds*, and directed and performed in Marc Blitzstein's *The Cradle Will Rock*. Subsequently, at the Curtis Institute of Music in Philadelphia, Bernstein studied piano with Isabella Vengerova, conducting with Fritz Reiner, and orchestration with Randall Thompson.

In 1940 Bernstein studied at the Boston Symphony Orchestra's newly created summer institute, Tanglewood, with the orchestra's conductor, Serge Koussevitzky. Bernstein later became Koussevitzky's conducting assistant. He made a sensational conducting debut with the New York Philharmonic in 1943. Bernstein became Music Director of the orchestra in 1958. From then until 1969 he led more concerts with the orchestra than any previous conductor. He subsequently held the lifetime title of Laureate Conductor, making frequent guest appearances with the orchestra. More than half of Bernstein's 400-plus recordings were made with the New York Philharmonic.

Bernstein traveled the world as a conductor. Immediately after World War II, in 1946, he conducted in London and at the International Music Festival in Prague. In 1947 he conducted in Tel Aviv, beginning a relationship with Israel that lasted until his death. In 1953 Bernstein was the first American to conduct opera at the Teatro alla Scala in Milan, in Cherubini's *Medea* with Maria Callas.

Beyond many distinguished achievements as a composer of concert works, Bernstein also wrote a one-act opera, *Trouble in Tahiti* (1952), and its sequel, the opera *A Quiet Place* (1983). He collaborated with choreographer Jerome Robbins on three major ballets: *Fancy Free* (1944), and *Facsimile* (1946) for American Ballet Theater, and *Dybbuk* (1974) for the New York City Ballet. Bernstein composed the score for the award-winning film *On the Waterfront* (1954) and incidental music for the Broadway play *The Lark* (1955).

Bernstein contributed substantially to the Broadway musical stage. He collaborated with Betty Comden and Adolph Green on *On the Town* (1944) and *Wonderful Town* (1953). For *Peter Pan* (1950) he penned his own lyrics to songs and also composed incidental music. In collaboration with Richard Wilbur, Lillian Hellman and others he wrote *Candide* (1956). Other versions of *Candide* were written in association with Hugh Wheeler, Stephen Sondheim and other lyricists. In 1957 he collaborated with Jerome Robbins, Stephen Sondheim and Arthur Laurents on the landmark musical *West Side Story*, which was made into an Academy Award-winning film. Bernstein also wrote the Broadway musical *1600 Pennsylvania Avenue* (1976) with lyricist Alan Jay Lerner.

In 1985 the National Academy of Recording Arts and Sciences honored Bernstein with the Lifetime Achievement Grammy Award. He won eleven Emmy Awards in his career. His televised concert and lecture series were launched with the "Omnibus" program in 1954, followed by the extraordinary "Young People's Concerts with the New York Philharmonic," which began in 1958 and extended over fourteen seasons. Among his many appearances on the PBS series "Great Performances" was the acclaimed eleven-part "Bernstein's Beethoven." In 1989 Bernstein and others commemorated the 1939 invasion of Poland in a worldwide telecast from Warsaw.

Bernstein's writings were published in *The Joy of Music* (1959), *Leonard Bernstein's Young People's Concerts* (1961), *The Infinite Variety of Music* (1966), and *Findings* (1982). Each has been widely translated. He gave six lectures at Harvard University in 1972-1973 as the Charles Eliot Norton Professor of Poetry. These lectures were subsequently published and televised as *The Unanswered Question*.

Bernstein received many honors. He was elected in 1981 to the American Academy of Arts and Letters, which gave him its Gold Medal. The National Fellowship Award in 1985 applauded his life-long support of humanitarian causes. He received the MacDowell Colony's Gold Medal; medals from the Beethoven Society and the Mahler Gesellschaft; the Handel Medallion, New York City's highest honor for the arts; a Tony award (1969) for Distinguished Achievement in the Theater; and dozens of honorary degrees and awards from colleges and universities. Bernstein was presented ceremonial keys to the cities of Oslo, Vienna, Bersheeva, and the village of Bernstein, Austria, among others. National honors came from Italy, Israel, Mexico, Denmark, Germany (the Great Merit Cross), and France (Chevalier, Officer and Commandeur of the Legion d'Honneur). Bernstein received the Kennedy Center Honors in 1980.

In 1990 Bernstein received the Praemium Imperiale, an international prize created in 1988 by the Japan Arts Association and awarded for lifetime achievement in the arts. He used the $100,000 prize to establish initiatives in the arts and education, principally the Leonard Bernstein Center for Artful Learning.

Bernstein was the father of three children — Jamie, Alexander and Nina — and enjoyed the arrival of his first two grandchildren, Francisca and Evan.

TABLE OF CONTENTS

Pianist on the recording: Jamie Johns

Notes on the Shows and Songs

FANCY FREE

Ballet. Music by Leonard Bernstein. First performance: American Ballet Theatre, April 18, 1944, Metropolitan Opera House, New York; Ballet Theatre Orchestra; Leonard Bernstein, conductor; Jerome Robbins, choreographer.

Selection:

Big Stuff

Choreographed by Jerome Robbins, *Fancy Free* was Bernstein's first ballet, which was an enormous success and is still regularly staged. The story, conceived by Robbins, is of three American Navy men on brief shore leave in New York City. The sailors meet women in a bar, and jealousies and fights occur. The concept was later expanded and altered for the musical *On the Town*. **"Big Stuff"** is heard on a juke box in the bar as the ballet opens. Bernstein wrote the song for Billie Holiday, but the producers could not afford her services. In 1945 Bernstein recorded "Big Stuff" with Billie Holiday, which was used as the introduction to the recording he conducted of *Fancy Free*. Bernstein himself sang the song for the 1979 recording he conducted of the ballet.

ON THE TOWN

Musical in two acts. Music by Leonard Bernstein. Lyrics by Betty Comden and Adolph Green. Book by Betty Comden and Adolph Green, based on an idea by Jerome Robbins. First performance: December 13, Boston. Broadway opening: December 28, 1944. Director of the original production: George Abbott. Choreographer: Jerome Robbins.

Selections:

I Can Cook Too

Some Other Time

Ain't Got No Tears Left (cut)

On the Town was the first Broadway musical success for a remarkable group of collaborators: Leonard Bernstein, lyricists/librettists Betty Comden and Adolph Green, and choreographer Jerome Robbins. Robbins and Bernstein had worked together in early 1944 on their ballet *Fancy Free*, which chronicled the one-day shore leave of three sailors in New York. By the spring they realized this material would make great musical comedy. Bernstein asked Comden and Green, his friends from a little known night-club act, to write the lyrics and book for the show. Veteran George Abbott directed the project. Bernstein wrote an entirely new score, not using any music from *Fancy Free*. Besides many inventive songs, the score featured musical passages that highlighted dazzling choreography by Robbins, which helped to further elevate the stature of dance on the Broadway stage. These interludes also showed Bernstein's unique, substantial theatre styles as a composer. Comden and Green brought their comic timing into their writing, realizing their own words in portraying the characters Claire and Ozzie onstage.

An American navy ship docks in New York during World War II. Three wide-eyed sailors disembark into the big city for the first time. They plan to cram their 24-hour shore leave full of sight-seeing and skirt-chasing. Chip wants to see all the sights, and Ozzie wants to meet some women. Gabey spies a poster of Ivy Smith in the subway, the new "Miss Turnstiles," the non-celebrity status of a young woman chosen to decorate the subway platforms each month. Along the way all three get sidetracked in a travelogue around New York. Chip finds he doesn't need the sight-seeing map given to him by his father after encountering boy-crazy lady cabbie, Hildy, who takes him back to her apartment claiming **"I Can Cook Too,"** in addition to her other gifts. Gabey, his friends and their new girlfriends head to Coney Island to find Ivy, who is performing there to earn money to pay her voice teacher, but are chased by the police. The two new couples, (Claire and Ozzie, and Hildy and Chip) realize their time together is running out in **"Some Other Time"** (originally a quartet, adapted as a solo for this edition). In the morning the sailors are "escorted" by New York's finest back to their ship.

The 1949 film version directed by Gene Kelly and Stanley Donen discarded most of Bernstein's score, retaining: "I Feel Like I'm Not Out of Bed Yet," "New York, New York" (adapted), "Miss Turnstiles Dance" (adapted), "Come Up to My Place," "A Day in New York Ballet" (adapted from "Times Square Ballet"), "Lonely Town," "Pas de Deux," and "Subway Ride and Imaginary Coney Island." Robbins' original choreography was replaced by Kelly and Donen.

PETER PAN

Play with music. Play by J.M. Barrie. Incidental music and lyrics by Leonard Bernstein. Broadway opening: April 24, 1950.

Selection:
Who Am I?

The character Peter Pan first appeared in a section of the 1902 novel *The Little White Bird* by Scottish writer J.M. Barrie (1860-1937). Barrie adapted the story for the stage in *Peter Pan, or The Boy Who Wouldn't Grow Up*, which was a big hit in London in 1904. Barrie again adapted the story and expanded it for the 1911 novel *Peter and Wendy*, later titled simply *Peter Pan*. The play became a popular classic in the UK and the US, with six Broadway productions between 1905 and 1928. A 1950 production, with movie star Jean Arthur as Peter, was its first in New York in 22 years. The production is decidedly a play with music, with songs and choruses, and not a full blown musical. It was originally intended as a musical, but the plan was made more modest due to the vocal limitations of Jean Arthur. *Peter Pan* has been the basis of many treatments, including a 1954 Mary Martin Broadway musical, completely different from the Bernstein version.

Lying in bed Wendy Darling wonders to herself **"Who Am I?"** as her two younger brothers are asleep. Peter Pan and his fairy Tinkerbell enter through the open window. Striking up a conversation with Wendy, Peter shows her and her brothers, Michael and John, how they can fly by thinking lovely, wonderful thoughts. Peter then leads the three children over the city of London, past the "second star to the right and straight on till morning" to the magical land of Neverland. Peter and all the other Lost Boys who don't want to grow up live a wonderful life of jungle adventures in a tree house. The Lost Boys cannot remember their mothers, so they want Wendy to stay on as theirs. Many adventures ensue as the children try to avoid the menacing Captain Hook. After a battle with Peter, Captain Hook is eaten by a crocodile. All the orphaned Lost Boys come to live with the Darling family, but Peter decides to stay in Neverland, remaining a boy forever.

WEST SIDE STORY

Musical in two acts. Music by Leonard Bernstein. Lyrics by Stephen Sondheim. Book by Arthur Laurents, loosely based on Shakespeare's *Romeo and Juliet*, based on a concept of Jerome Robbins. First performance: August 19, 1957, Washington, D.C. Broadway opening: September 26, 1957. Original production directed and choreographed by Jerome Robbins.

Selection:

Somewhere

The origins of *West Side Story* can be traced to early 1949. Jerome Robbins, who had conceived *On the Town*, approached Leonard Bernstein about a re-imagining and updating of *Romeo and Juliet*. The initial concept involved a Jewish boy and an Italian Catholic girl on New York's lower east side. Bernstein was interested, along with Arthur Laurents, but Bernstein had other commitments. In 1955 the three picked up the idea again, changing the players in the tale to reflect the mid-1950s mood and the issues over Puerto Rican immigration into the city. With the idea of rival gangs, moved to the New York neighborhood of gang activity at the time, *West Side Story* was off and running. A young Stephen Sondheim was brought in to write lyrics. The authors tried to usher in a new kind of American drama with *West Side Story*, not quite opera, but not quite traditional Broadway musical, with a stronger emphasis on character and dance. Bernstein later stated, "I don't consider it an opera. I think it has operatic qualities and moments, but it's not an opera because it is basically spoken dialogue scenes interspersed with music, even though it's much more interspersed than the average… I think what distinguishes *West Side Story* from other musicals is the copious use of dance, and this provides simply twice as much music as you ordinarily hear."

The show portrays a struggle for the streets of New York between two gangs. The Jets, a group of self-styled "American" teenagers, are led by Riff. The Sharks, Puerto Rican newcomers, are led by the fiery Bernardo. This bitter rivalry has deep seeds in racial prejudice and cultural insensitivity. Both the Sharks and the Jets and their girls attend a dance at a school gym, where Tony meets and falls in love at first sight with Maria, Bernardo's sister. A plan for a showdown rumble is made between the two gangs. Tony persuades them that it will be a fair fistfight rather than something more violent with weapons. That evening things get out of hand at the rumble. Bernardo draws a switchblade and fatally stabs Riff. Impulsively acting in shock, grief and anger Tony stabs and kills Bernardo in instant revenge.

Tony comes to Maria, anguished. Maria's love for him wins over her grief for her brother's death. They dream of a safe and peaceful place, which appears in a ballet sequence. A young woman (the character is simply called "A Girl") sings **"Somewhere"** about the hope for such a place before the return to reality. Tony slips away. Anita reluctantly agrees to take a message for Maria, detained by police for questioning, to Tony at Doc's drugstore, where she is manhandled and nearly raped by the Jets. In anger she lies and tells them that Chino has found out about Tony and Maria, and has killed Maria. Unconsolable at the news, Tony rushes in the street, yelling for Chino to shoot him. Just as he sees Maria a shot rings out, and Tony soon lies dying in Maria's arms.

Most of the score was retained for the 1961 film version of the musical, although there were drastic shifts in song and scene order.

WONDERFUL TOWN

Musical in two acts. Music by Leonard Bernstein. Lyrics by Betty Comden and Adolph Green. Book by Joseph A. Fields and Jerome Chodorov, based on their play *My Sister Eileen*. First performance: January 19, 1953, New Haven, Connecticut. Broadway opening: February 26, 1953.

Selections:

One Hundred Easy Ways to Lose a Man

The Story of My Life (cut)

The 1940 play *My Sister Eileen* was based on semi-autobiographical stories by Ruth McKenney that appeared in *The New Yorker*. Rosalind Russell played the role of Ruth Sherwood in the 1942 Columbia Pictures movie of *My Sister Eileen*. A few years later the musical *Wonderful Town* was written as a stage vehicle for her. Initially other writers were engaged. When they failed to impress the producers, Bernstein, Comden and Green were brought in to write music and lyrics. Under pressure to finish before the producer's option on Russell's contract expired, the team turned out the score in four weeks.

In the 1930s Ruth and Eileen are two sisters making their way in Greenwich Village, having recently moved from Ohio. Ruth is trying to be a writer (she has a typewriter, at least), and Eileen struggles to become an actress (her principal talent is that she's pretty). Eileen gets along smartly with every man she meets, while tomboyish, assertive Ruth thinks she should switch her angle to writing stories on **"One Hundred Easy Ways to Lose a Man."** Ruth's potential editor at the *Manhatter*, Bob Baker, tells her she should move back west before he even looks at her writing. After reading her stories he comes to see Ruth at home to apologize for being curt, and instead encounters Eileen, who immediately falls a little bit in love with him. Later, Eileen realizes that Ruth loves Bob, and suddenly Bob realizes, despite wanting a quiet girl, he's in love with the boisterous Ruth. Ruth and Bob find one another, and forbidding New York has turned out to be a wonderful town.

The cut song "The Story of My Life," written for the character Ruth, was included in the 1975 Off-Broadway revue *By Bernstein* (withdrawn by the composer).

SONGS IN A THEATRE STYLE NOT FROM A SHOW

Another Love

Music and lyrics by Leonard Bernstein. Lyrics by Betty Comden and Adolph Green.

Composition date unknown. The reason for writing the song, and its possible place in a show is also not known. "Another Love" was included in the 1975 Off-Broadway revue *By Bernstein* (withdrawn by the composer).

It's Gotta Be Bad to Be Good

Music and lyrics by Leonard Bernstein.

It is believed to have been written in the 1940s, but the reason for writing the song and its possible place in a show is not known. "It's Gotta Be Bad to Be Good" was included in the 1975 Off-Broadway revue *By Bernstein* (withdrawn by the composer).

Big Stuff
from the ballet *Fancy Free*
original key

Words and Music by
LEONARD BERNSTEIN

Slow and blue

So you cry, "What's it a - bout, __ Ba - by?"

You ask why the blues had to go and pick you. __

So you go down to the shore, __ kid stuff;

* This is Bernstein's original rhythmic notation. All eighth-notes are performed (♪♪ = ♪ ♪).

Don't you know there's hon - ey in store __ for you,

Big Stuff? __ Let's take a ride in my gra-vy train; The door's o-pen wide,

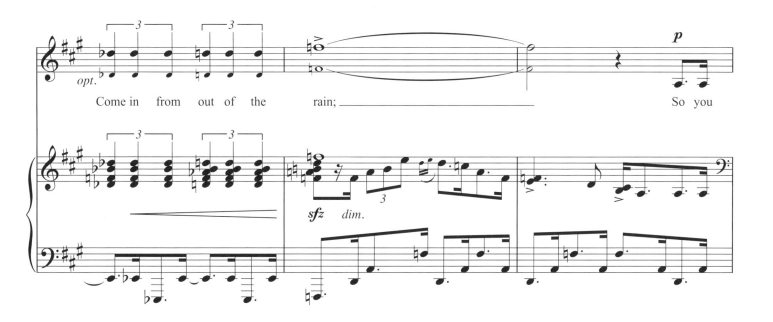

Come in from out of the rain; __ So you

stare, call it de - spair, ___ Ba - by; Don't you care?

I'm on the square a - bout you; Let's have a try; it may be that

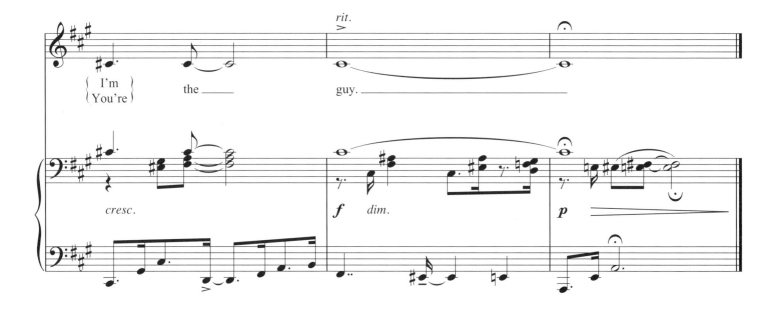

$\left\{ \begin{array}{l} I'm \\ You're \end{array} \right\}$ the ___ guy. ___

Ain't Got No Tears Left

cut from *On the Town*

original key: F Major

Music and Lyrics by
LEONARD BERNSTEIN

The day you walked out with-out an-y trace _ I tried to find you, but

you won the race, _ And now I sit here, don't go an-y-place, _ Just keep on

star-in' in-to space Re-mem-ber-in' your face. Ain't got no hope _ I'm gon-na

find you some day, _ Won't be to-night, _ Won't be to-mor-row.

I Can Cook Too

from *On the Town*

original key

Lyrics by
BETTY COMDEN and ADOLPH GREEN

Music by
LEONARD BERNSTEIN

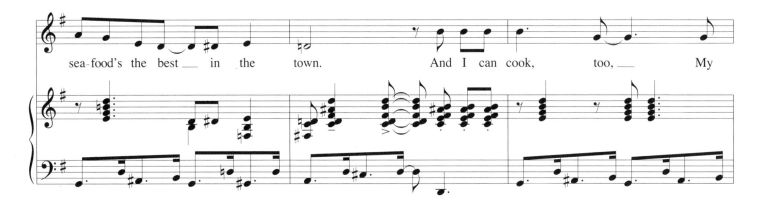

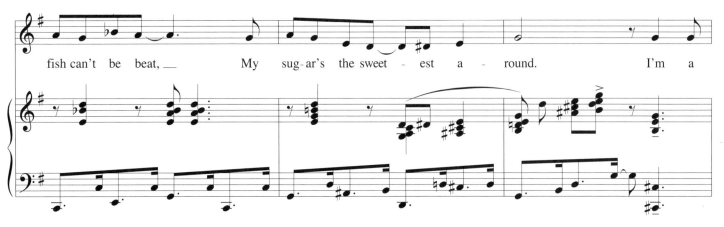

Oh, I can cook, too, — on top of the rest, — My sea-food's the best — in the town. And I can cook, too, — My fish can't be beat, — My sug-ar's the sweet-est a-round. I'm a

man's i - deal of a per - fect meal, __ Right down to the dem - i - tasse. __

__ I'm a pot of joy for a hun - gry boy, __

Ba - by, I'm cook-ing with gas! __ Oh, I'm a gum - drop, __ A

fz

sweet lol - li - pop, __ A brook trout right out __ of the brook, __ And

cresc.

what's more, ba - by, I ____ can cook! ____

Some girls make mag - a - zine cov - ers, Some girls keep house on a dime, ____

Some girls make won - der - ful lov - ers, But what a luck - y find I'm. ____

Light rhythm

I'd make a mag-a-zine cov - er, I do keep

house on a dime, ___ I'd make a won-der-ful lov - er,

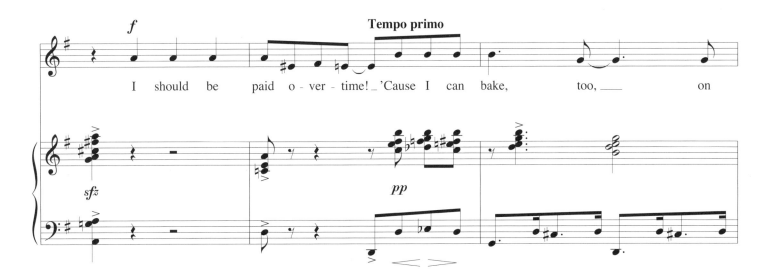

I should be paid o-ver-time! 'Cause I can bake, too, ___ on

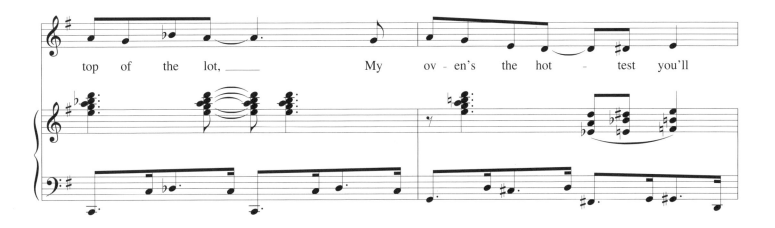

top of the lot, ___ My ov-en's the hot - test you'll

find. Yes, I can roast, too, __ My chick-ens just ooze, __ My

gra - vy will lose _____ you your mind. I'm a

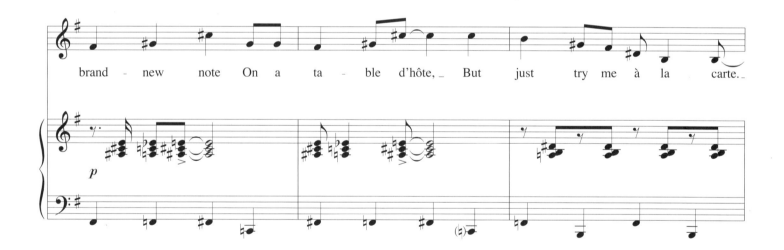

brand - new note On a ta - ble d'hôte, _ But just try me à la carte.

_____ With a sin - gle course, You could choke a horse. __

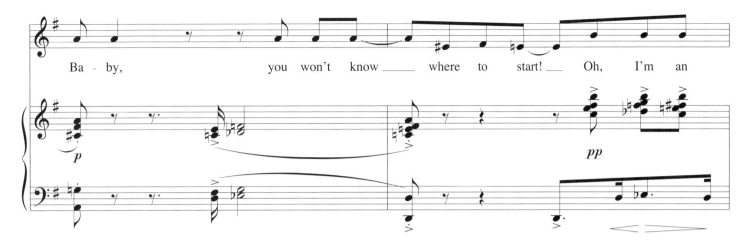

Ba - by, you won't know where to start! Oh, I'm an

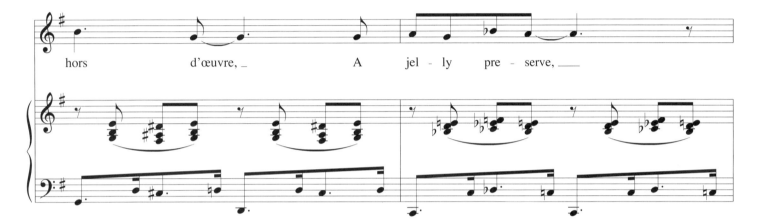

hors d'œuvre, A jel - ly pre - serve,

Not in the re - ci - pe book, And what's more,

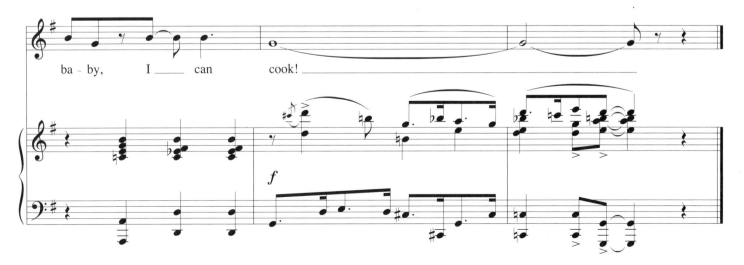

ba - by, I can cook!

Some Other Time

from *On the Town*

original key: a major 3rd higher

Lyrics by
BETTY COMDEN and ADOLPH GREEN

Music by
LEONARD BERNSTEIN

Begun by Claire, this song becomes a quartet in the show for Claire, Hildy, Chip and Ozzie. Adapted as a solo for this edition.

time is rac-ing. Oh, well, we'll catch up Some oth-er time. _____

Just when the fun is start-ing Comes the time for part-ing But let's be glad for

what we've had, And what's to come. There's so much more em-brac-ing

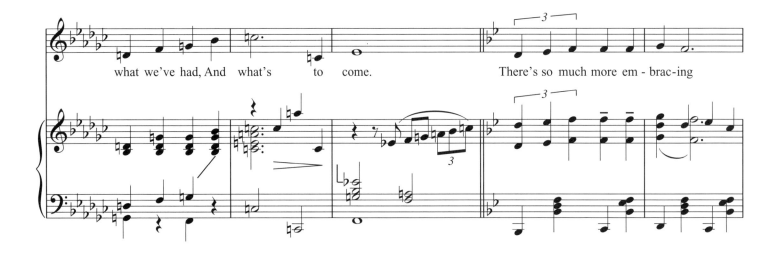

Still to be done, but time is rac-ing, Oh, well, We'll catch up Some oth-er time. _____

Who Am I?

from *Peter Pan*

original key

Words and Music by
LEONARD BERNSTEIN

Refrain

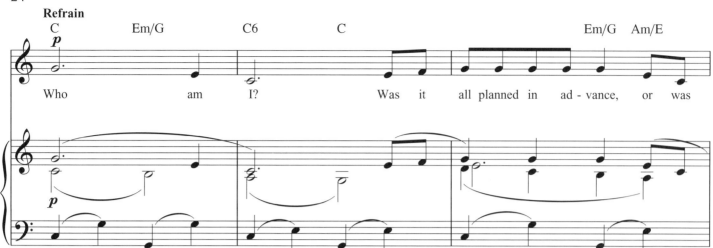

Who am I? Was it all planned in ad-vance, or was

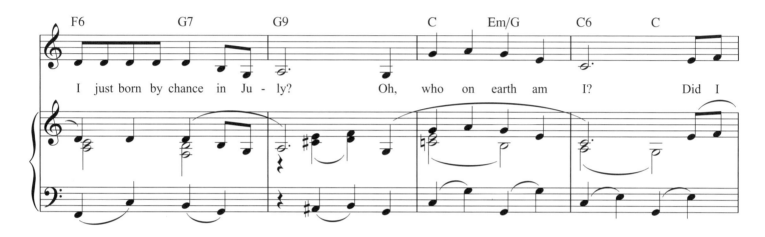

I just born by chance in Ju-ly? Oh, who on earth am I? Did I

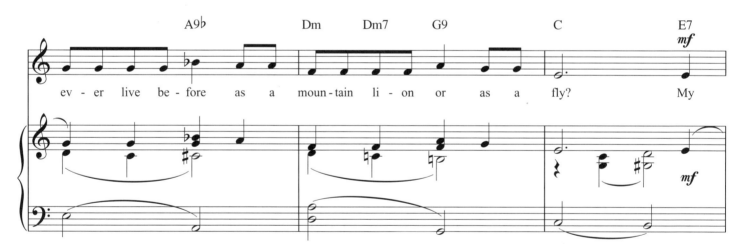

ev-er live be-fore as a moun-tain li-on or as a fly? My

friends on-ly think of fun; They're all such in-cur-a-ble tots! Can

I be the on-ly one who thinks these mys-ter-i-ous thoughts? Some

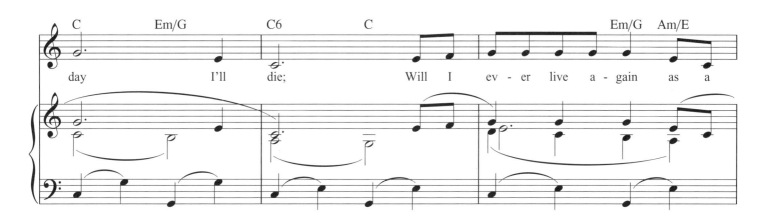

day I'll die; Will I ev-er live a-gain as a

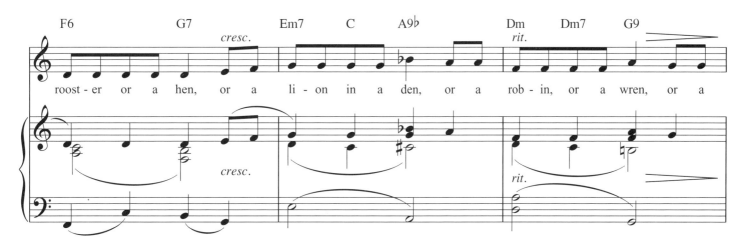

roost-er or a hen, or a li-on in a den, or a rob-in, or a wren, or a

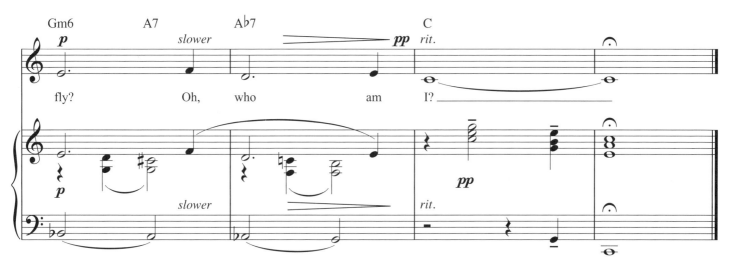

fly? Oh, who am I?

Somewhere
from *West Side Story*
original key: E Major

Lyrics by
STEPHEN SONDHEIM

Music by
LEONARD BERNSTEIN

In the show the song is sung by a character simply known as "A Girl."

A time and place for us. Hold my hand and we're half - way there.

cresc. *f*

Hold my hand and I'll take you there Some - how,_____

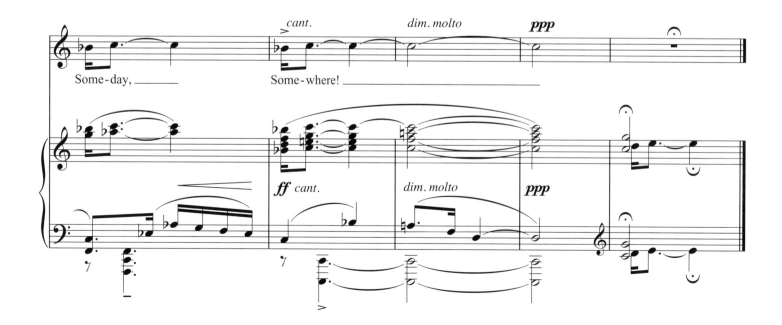

cant. *dim. molto* *ppp*

Some - day,_____ Some - where!_____

Leonard Bernstein®

One Hundred Easy Ways to Lose a Man

from *Wonderful Town*

original key

Lyrics by
BETTY COMDEN and ADOLPH GREEN

Music by
LEONARD BERNSTEIN

(Spoken flatly)
Just leap out, crawl under
the car, say it's the gasket,
and fix it in two seconds flat
with a bobby pin.

rall.

bat your eyes and say, "What __ a ro - man - tic spot we're in." __

a tempo

That's a good way to lose __ a man. __ He takes you to a base - ball game, you

sit knee to knee. __ He says, "The next man up at bat will bunt, you'll see." __ Don't

Just say, "Bunt? Are you nuts?!
With no outs, two men on base, and
a left-handed batter coming up, he'll
walk right into a triple play, just
like it happened in the fifth game
of the World Series in 1923."

rall.

say, "Oooh, what's a bunt? This game's too hard for lit - tle me." __

a tempo   **Faster (but light)**

That's a sure way to lose ___ a man. ___ A sure, sure, sure, sure

way to lose a man, A splen-did way ___ to lose a man. ___ Just throw your

Tempo I

know-ledge in his face, He'll nev-er try for sec-ond base.

(spoken)   *(sung)*

Nine-ty-eight ways to go. The third way to lose ___ a man: ___ The

whis - pers, "You're the one to who I give my heart." __ Don't say, "I love you, too, my dear, let's

Just say, "I'm afraid you've made a grammatical
error. It's not "To who I give my heart," it's
"To whom I give my heart." -- You see,
with the use of the preposition "to," "who"
becomes the indirect object, making the use of
"whom" imperative; which I can easily
show you by drawing a simple chart."

nev - er, nev - er part." __ That's a fine way to lose __ a man. __ A

Tempo II (Faster)

fine, fine, fine, fine way to lose a man, A dan - dy way _____ to lose a

Slow and free

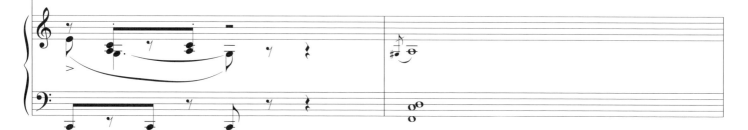

man. __ Just be more well in - formed than he, You'll nev - er

The Story of My Life

cut from *Wonderful Town*

original key

Lyrics by
BETTY COMDEN and ADOLPH GREEN

Music by
LEONARD BERNSTEIN

You wake one day, the sun is bright. You feel like strol-ling through the town.

Your dress is new, your hat just right _____ and then the rain comes pour-ing down.

Well, that's the sto-ry of my life. You dream you've heard a love-ly song,

All night you're haunt-ed by its theme. When you wake up, the notes are wrong. _____ The song has van-ished with the dream. Well, that's the sto-ry of my life. Like an-y sto-ry that is filled with love and joy and hope as it grows. And then the sto-ry ends with-out the love, the joy the hope, at the

38

little thing happened to me the other night, on my way down to the lower depths. I was on this blind date; it was awful.

(improvise in a cocktail style)
a tempo

Then in no time at all I could see as far as he was concerned, the blind date was me.   Well, that's the sto-ry of my

life.   I went to my office the other day. I have this crush on my big, handsome boss, this curly-headed dream. To get him is my

scheme. For five years, nothing happened. Then one day, I just happened to take off my glasses, and he said: *(screaming)* "Aaaagh!"
(normal voice) I have some advice
for you younger girls: stay younger.

rall.

So it goes. You leave the life you've al-ways known,

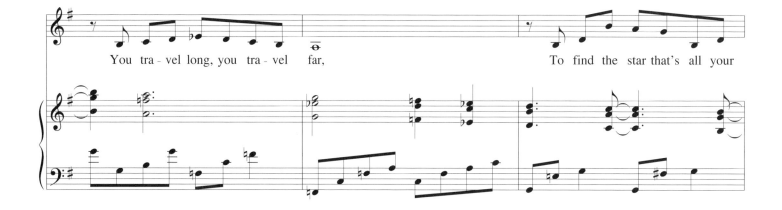

You tra-vel long, you tra-vel far, To find the star that's all your

own, ___ But then you nev-er find the star. Well, that's the sto-ry of my

life, The clas-sic sto-ry of my life.

Another Love

original key: F Major

Lyrics by
BETTY COMDEN and ADOLPH GREEN

Music by
LEONARD BERNSTEIN

Slow and bluesy (slow swing beat)

and so I've had an-oth-er love, _

and so I've had an-oth-er love. ___

It's Gotta Be Bad to Be Good

original key

Words and Music by
LEONARD BERNSTEIN

You don't talk to me ten - der, or treat me ea - sy, the way that a good __ lov - er should. It's not ver - y gay __ but

love is that way. ___ It's got-ta be bad ___ to be good. ___ Since the

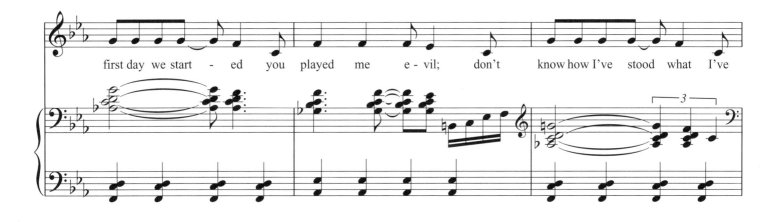

first day we start-ed you played me e-vil; don't know how I've stood what I've

stood, but I'll stay a-round ___ 'cause ba-by I've found it's

got-ta be bad ___ to be good. ___ You say that I'll leave you, bad

pen - ny, bye - bye, ___ that I'll go and de - ceive you with

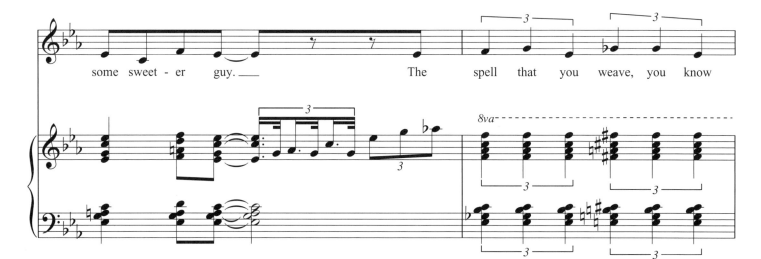

some sweet - er guy. ___ The spell that you weave, you know

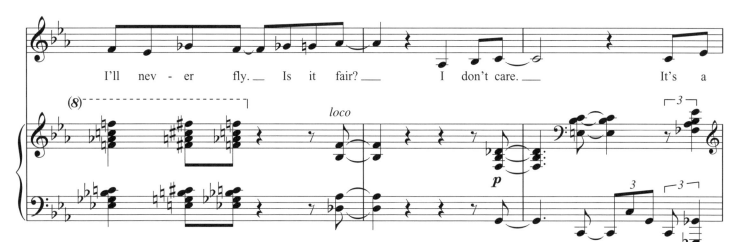

I'll nev - er fly. ___ Is it fair? ___ I don't care. ___ It's a

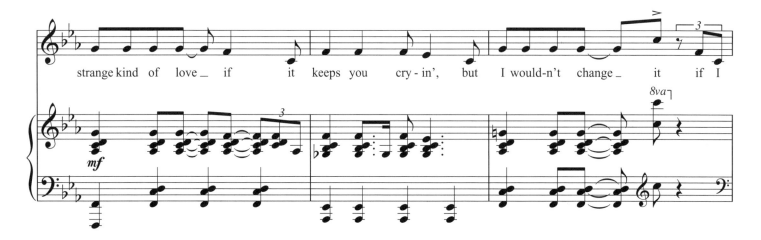

strange kind of love ___ if it keeps you cry - in', but I would-n't change ___ it if I

could.   I'm   in   for   a   ride, ___   but

I'm   sat-is-fied, ___ 'cause it's   got-ta be   bad ___   to be good. ___   'Cause it's

got-ta   be   bad, ___   'cause if love is-n't bad ___   it ain't

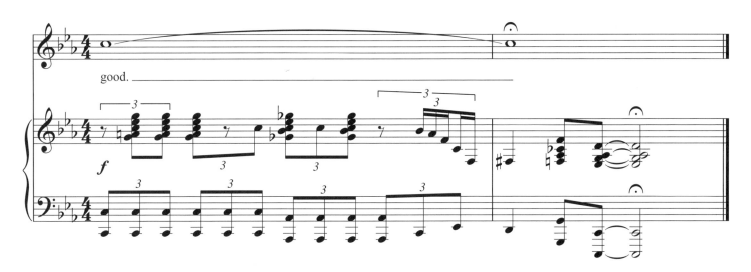

good. _____